like a tree

BY DICK BERNAL

like a tree

Copyright © 2017 by Dick Bernal

All Rights Reserved. This book is protected under the copy-right laws of the United States of America. This book and any portion thereof may not be copied or reprinted for commercial gain or profit. The use of short quotations or occasional page copying for personal or group study is permitted and encouraged.

Scripture quotations are from the New King James Version of the Holy Bible, copyright 1991 by Thomas Nelson, Inc.

ISBN# 13-978-0692931837

Printed in the United States of America

Published by
Jubilee Christian Center
175 Nortech Parkway
San Jose, California 95134
www.jubilee.org

CONTENTS

INTRODUCTION	7
THE REDWOODS	11
THE OAK	17
THE EUCALYPTUS · THE IMMIGRANT TREE	21
THE PALM TREE	27
THE PARABLE OF THE TREES	31
THE PINES OF CALIFORNIA	35
THE HOLY TREES OF THE BIBLE	41
THE ACACIA	42
CEDARS OF LEBANON	43
THE MONTEREY CYPRESS	47
EDEN'S TREES	51
THE TREE OF THE KNOWLEDGE OF GOOD AND EVIL	54
THE SYCAMINE TREE	59
THE SYCAMORE TREE	65
CONCLUSION	71

> *We need to find God, and He cannot be found in noise and restlessness.*
> *God is the friend of silence.*
> *See how nature - trees, flowers, grass - grows in silence; see the stars, the moon and the sun, how they move in silence...*
> *We need silence to be able to touch souls.*

Mother Teresa

INTRODUCTION

Here's a question. If you were a tree what kind of tree would you want to be? I know my choice, which I will reveal in the opening chapter.

I love the colorful language and metaphors in the Bible. As a new believer hungry to understand what was in my first Bible my wife Carla bought for me back in 1977, I soon discovered this is not a boring, scientific journal, but a beautiful collection of stories, psalms, proverbs, letters, and books. At times, the Bible is prophetic, historical, and even poetic.

Something else that caught my attention was how many of the various authors used images, similes, and metaphors to help us better understand the mysteries of God, and His Kingdom. The New Testament has nearly a hundred of these with the parables of Jesus as examples. We believers are likened to sheep in one place, yet told to be *wise as a serpent, yet gentle as a dove,* in another.

"Blessed is the man who walks not in the counsel of the ungodly, nor stands in the path of sinners, nor sits in the seat of the scornful; but his delight is in the law of the Lord, and in His law, he meditates day and night. He shall be like a tree planted by the rivers of water, that brings forth its fruit in its season, whose leaf also shall not wither; and whatever he does shall prosper." — Psalm 1:1-3

In the Old Testament, we are encouraged to be like eagles; and in the New Testament, borrowing from nature, the Bible uses a vineyard, salt and light, fruit, and seed to help us understand God's Kingdom principles.

In one place, we are described as an army with armor and weapons, and in another place, we are a bride (I told my wife I don't mind a wedding dress as long as I can wear boots and carry a rifle). The Holy Spirit, who understands our mind and how it processes information and pictures brilliantly reveals God's unseen realm with images we can easily relate to.

LIKE A TREE!

Of all the interesting metaphors in the Bible, I chose to write a few life lessons from some of my favorite trees. Enjoy!

> *The Redwoods, once seen, leave a mark or create a vision that stays with you always.*

John Steinbeck

THE REDWOODS
Chapter 1

Growing up in Northern California, I've always had a fondness for trees. Around our neighborhood in Watsonville where I spent my early childhood years were scores of Apple Orchards. For a while, Watsonville was known as *The Apple Town of California*. We kids would play Army, Cowboys and Indians, and Hide-N-Go Seek amongst the orchards, well at least until the owner and his dogs would chase us off. Down by Pinto Lake were Elm and Maple trees big enough to build a tree fort and pretend we were everyone from Tarzan to Robin Hood. Trees were always a big part of my adolescence.

Every summer my family made two camping trips. One, to close by Mount Madonna Park up in the Santa Cruz range, only fifteen miles from where we lived and, two, to Yosemite Valley, a couple of hundred miles East of Watsonville. Mount Madonna has beautiful coastal Redwoods mixed in with other indigenous species. Now, on the way to Yosemite was another kind of Redwood tree that, even to this day, drops my jaw. The giant Sequoia! These behemoths can grow as big as a skyscraper. One that was unfortunately cut down during the gold rush was so big they turned the stump into a dance floor. I remember as a kid driving our 1948 Pontiac through a tunnel carved out of one. We kids thought these monster trees were the coolest. They can live up to three thousand years.

One old tree had a sign saying it was a baby Redwood when King David started his reign. As old as these can be, there's one still older in California, and it's arguably the oldest of all trees, the *Methuselah!* It's a Bristlecone Pine from California's white mountains. Experts think it to be almost five thousand years old, which makes it the oldest non-clonal tree in the world. Its exact location is a forest service secret for obvious reasons.

If I were a tree, I think I'd like to be a Redwood. I have reasons beyond its longevity.

The biggest tree in the world is the General Sherman. This beauty is 275 feet tall and one hundred feet wide at its trunk and very, very old, yet healthy.

General Sherman is the king of the forest. Thanks to John Muir, American naturalist, environmentalist, and author, we have this magical forest as a national park today and thousands of species of trees still with us.

To be clear, not all Redwoods are Sequoias. However, all Redwoods come from the same family, the giant Coastal Redwoods, found just North of San Francisco and also up near the Oregon border, and are slightly different than the Sequoias.

Here's an interesting fact about Redwood trees: they need fire to regenerate. Most trees are destroyed by forest fires, but not Redwood trees. They *need* fire! The heat triggers a unique response from the tree. It drops its cones in mass up to a thousand-five hundred per tree. The heat from the fire cause the cones to pop open, which helps the seeds be released to find a home. Forest fires also get rid of underbrush and other species that are competing for life. The ash that's remaining is a great fertilizer for those newly released seeds.

Another interesting fact about Redwoods is they have *thick skin.* The bark of one of these giants can be up to two feet thick. The natural enemies of the forest, in general, are insects, fungi, and fire. Up in the Sierra's of Northern California, you will find brown dying Pine trees that stand out like a sore thumb amongst the beautiful green ones.

What kills these is called the Pine beetle. The Redwood is too tough to be taken down by the Beelzebub of the forest. The brutal winters of the Sierra's, with several feet of snow too, help preserve these *soldiers of the forest.* The snow and ice kill off potential life-threatening enemies to these majestic, natural works of art.

Be like a tree planted by living waters! No matter what the devil or life throws at you, you will not fall.

"In this you greatly rejoice, though now for a little while, if need be, you have been grieved by various trials, that the genuineness of your faith, being much more precious than gold that perishes, though it is tested by fire, may be found to praise, honor, and glory at the revelation of Jesus Christ."
— 1 Peter 1:6-7

> *A large Oak Tree is just a little nut that refused to give up.*

David McGee

THE OAK
Chapter 2

My second favorite tree is the Oak tree (Genus Quercus). There are over six hundred species of Oak trees around the world. I'm most acquainted with the California Oaks that dot my valley and the Eastern foothills.

There are several reasons I love oaks. None of them look alike. From their hearty, strong trunk to the gnarled branches and shiny little leaves, these beauties are eye catchers.

Here in the Bay Area, to have one in your yard, front or back, increases the value of your house.

Our local Oaks can live up to three hundred years, but other species around the world have lived nearly a thousand years.

In the Bible, Oak trees are called by different names, like in Genesis 12:6, where they are called *Terebinth trees*. About five other Hebrew words are used to describe the Oak trees of different regions.

In Biblical times, and to this day, the wood (hardwood) of Oak trees is useful and desirable in making floors, cabinets, paneling, and furniture to name a few. The various warm colors of Oakwood make it pleasant to the eye.

I have a habit of collecting acorns from Oak trees. I always keep a few on my desk at home as a reminder that inside every acorn is potentially a beautiful Oak tree.

Having pastored thousands of people for almost forty years, I have often found myself wondering what's inside trying to get out of the folks I pastor! Like the acorn that becomes a mature tree, many factors come into play. A large mature Oak tree can drop up to ten thousand acorns a year. Where I live, most acorns are gathered by squirrels, or eaten by wild boars or some other acorn-loving critters. Needless to say, very few ever become Oak trees.

I live in Silicon Valley, the epicenter of cognitive innovation. It's a virtual incu-bator for the *new and next*. Yet, with the thousands of ideas floating around this magic kingdom, very few turn into a world-class company like Apple. Acorns need a lot of things to be *just right* to sprout and grow. Oak trees, like the Redwoods, are strong and hearty. They can withstand severe weather, killer insects, and drought.

The taproot of the Oak tree is only 18 feet from the surface. But the lateral roots can spread out horizontally more than seven times the width of the crown of the tree, searching for water and needful nutrients.

Years ago, I was going through the biggest crisis of my ministry. A friend called to pray with me and encourage me. He said, "Pastor Dick, you're an Oak. Nothing's taking you down. Stand strong." Funny, after that phone call I drove by one of my favorite old Oaks close to my house. I got out of my car and just stared at it. I thought, *Yep, I'll be ok,* and I was.

> Even the giant Eucalyptus tree has had some humble beginnings as a two-leaved seedling.

The Floral World

THE EUCALYPTUS
THE IMMIGRANT TREE
Chapter 3

In the Northern part of California, one doesn't have to go far to see Eucalyptus trees, or, as they are called from *down under,* Blue Gum trees. A few years back I was in Sydney, Australia speaking at a conference and I had a few days off to go exploring. My host had a thirty-three foot sailboat, and he took my wife and me on a cruise around the area. Everywhere we looked we saw stands of Blue Gums. Some were two-hundred feet tall.

It's easy to see why they are called Blue Gums. They have waxy blue leaves and smooth, grayish bark. When the bark is peeled off it reveals a yellowish, pink surface. I've always enjoyed these immigrants from Australia. We have several on our church property, and where I play golf they are hard to miss — literally! The way I play, I've hit many Blue Gums with errant drives.

How did Eucalyptus come to California? Maybe a better question is *why* were these brought to California? In 1770, Eucalyptus (Greek for *well covered*) made their way to Europe for the first time. The exotic look of these Blue Gums caught the fancy of many upper class Europeans, and to have one or more of the many varieties of these strange but beautiful looking trees was a feather in the cap.

The legendary Captain James Cook first brought them to London, England, for botanists to study. Australian landowners found a new *cash cow* with the growing demand for the plenteous Gums they had growing on their properties. The Aussies had over six hundred species, from smallish, bush-like ones that I have in my backyard, to majestic skyscraper varieties that can grow to a height of two hundred feet.

When I was in high school, I had a summer job at a Eucalyptus nursery where the owner had over two hundred species.

My favorite was the silver dollar. The leaves naturally looked like silver dollars.

What brought them to California? Gold! The gold rush brought fortune seekers, merchants, and builders from various trades, and a host of folks anxious to go west. With the boom of 1849, the need for wood and lumber greatly increased. Deforestation and strip mining became a concern to the point, in 1868, the Tree Culture Act was passed.

People were encouraged to plant more trees. This is where the Eucalyptus came into play. Business-minded entrepreneurs, like Elmwood Cooper, seized upon the moment to start large scale commercial planting with hopes of getting his foot first in the door of a potentially vast lumber market. But soon the truth exposed a weakness. In his and other investor's plans: the old growth Gums in Australia, after one hundred and fifty to two hundred years, developed hard wood like Oak trees. But young, California Eucalyptus trees were soft and of no use in the building trades. So, they had to find other uses for the immigrant trees.

In Central and Northern California, you can spot miles and miles of Eucalyptus along roads in agricultural areas. These trees act as windbreaks protecting valuable crops. Later, scientists found the leaves of the Eucalyptus have healing properties and other uses like air fresheners; even its oil is used in industrial mining. The aboriginals have known the healing power of Gum leaves for thousands of years.

Most of us are immigrants to one degree or another, like the Eucalyptus tree. My people are from Spain, then Mexico (Sinaloa area), and in the 1800's they traveled up to California.

They thought they were settling this land for the Spanish Empire, but in 1850 California became the thirty-first state of the union. Obviously, things changed.

Perhaps like a beautiful Gum tree, you thought you were brought to where you are for one reason, but a new reason with a new season has emerged.

At times, I get frustrated living and pastoring in the San Francisco Bay Area. Toto, this ain't Kansas! Nevertheless,

I believe I was born here, and live here, and I serve in the ministry here for such a time as this.

Stay planted where God put you and continue to drink from living water.

❝

It is the nature of the strong heart, that like the Palm Tree it strives ever upwards when it is most burdened.

❞

Philip Sidney

THE PALM TREE
Chapter 4

What comes to mind when you see or think about Palm trees? Hawaii? Southern California or Palm Springs? Maybe an oasis in the Middle East? There are over 2,600 species of the *Arecaceae,* the Palm's scientific name.

We have a Christian celebration called *Palm Sunday* the week before Easter. In Judaism, Palms represent *peace and plenty or prosperity,* and the ancient city of Jericho is called *The city of Palm trees.*

I like this Psalm:

"The righteous shall flourish like a palm tree, He shall grow like a cedar in Lebanon. Those who are planted in the house of the Lord shall flourish in the courts of our God. They shall still bear fruit in old age; they shall be fresh and flourishing." — Psalm 92:12-14

The Palm trees that are mentioned many times in the Bible were probably Date Palms. I love dates! I also love coconuts, which, of course come from a different species that grow in tropical areas. Recently, we Americans have discovered lots of staples made with palm oil that comes from the fruit of the Oil Palm tree.

Where did the Palm tree get its name? Hold up your arm (tree trunk) and spread your fingers (leaves) and you look like a Palm tree.

Like the Redwood and the Eucalyptus, one particular species, the Quindio Wax Palm in Colombia, South America, can grow up to two hundred feet tall.

The Romans of old revered the Palm tree. Their branches were symbols of victory and triumph, which probably upset them as Jesus rode into town with the crowd waving palm branches.

What amazes me is how delicate a Palm tree can look in regions where hurricanes or typhoons are likely to hit, and yet these skinny, tall, fibrous beauties can *go with the flow*, and bend like rubber, but not break. They are one of the toughest trees on earth.

In my backyard, I have three species of Palms. Recently we had a freeze, which is abnormal for our area. Afterwards, I noticed some of the branches of many of my palms had turned blackish. I thought, *"Oh no! My beautiful Palms who love hot weather are done for."* Well, hang on a minute. My gardener pruned away the damaged branches, and almost overnight new ones sprang forth. I love comeback stories!

Yes, I wouldn't mind being likened to a Palm tree.

"

Consider a tree for a moment. As beautiful as trees are to look at, we don't see what goes on underground — as they grow roots. Trees must develop deep roots in order to grow strong and produce their beauty. But we don't see the roots. We just see and enjoy the beauty. In much the same way, what goes on inside of us is like the roots of a tree.

"

Joyce Meyer

THE PARABLE OF THE TREES
Chapter 5

" Now when they told Jotham, he went and stood on top of Mount Gerizim, and lifted his voice and cried out. And he said to them: "Listen to me, you men of Shechem, That God may listen to you!

" The trees once went forth to anoint a king over them. And they said to the olive tree, 'Reign over us!' But the olive tree said to them, 'Should I cease giving my oil, With which they honor God and men, And go to sway over trees?'

> "Then the trees said to the fig tree, 'You come and reign over us!' But the fig tree said to them, 'Should I cease my sweetness and my good fruit, And go to sway over trees?'
> "Then the trees said to the vine, 'You come and reign over us!' But the vine said to them, 'Should I cease my new wine, which cheers both God and men, and go to sway over trees?'
>
> "Then all the trees said to the bramble, 'You come and reign over us!' and the bramble said to the trees, 'If in truth you anoint me as king over you, then come and take shelter in my shade; But if not, let fire come out of the bramble and devour the cedars of Lebanon!'" — Judges 9:7-15

This is the first parable in the Bible. Of course, much later our Lord will do much of His teachings in parable form. A parable can be a metaphor, a proverb, a poem, or a simile. Middle Eastern culture loved telling or hearing parables. Jesus used these fictitious narratives from common life to convey a moral truth or a kingdom view.

Three of my favorite trees from the Bible are given a voice in our text: the Olive, the Fig, and the Vine. What I like about this parable is that all of the trees know their place, their calling, and their purpose. They humbly refuse to be tempted by power and position.

The three trees know there is only one King and He is God Almighty. They know their very existence and blessing to produce fruit that is useful and delightful is from their creator. All through the Word of God, we see examples of olives, olive branches, and olive oil. Likewise, the fig was a favorite fruit for consumption. And yes, the Vine tree, with its wonderful grapes and wine has put many a smile on countless faces for millenniums.

In verse fifteen, the bramble, which is not a tree but a useless bush, jumps at the opportunity for power and privilege! It's also called the Thorn bush. The bramble bush produces no fruit. Its only use was firewood.

What do I take away from this story? Stay in your lane! Stay where God has planted you! Promotion comes from the Lord. Keep producing fruit and good fruit, don't compete with the other trees but complete one another.

> *God took pattern after a
> Pine Tree and built you noble.*
>
> Zora Neale Hursten

THE PINES OF CALIFORNIA
Chapter 6

I grew up in a camping family. After WWII, Army surplus stores had an abundance of tents and tools that are handy for camping. My Grandpa, Grandma, Mom, my two sisters and I all loved being in the woods. To me, it was a grand adventure.

My favorite spot to camp was Yosemite Valley. Every summer we headed up to the High Sierras for two weeks. We would leave the Bay Area and drive east across the Big Valley. It took a few hours before we began to climb the western slope of the Sierras.

I remember rolling the backseat window down so I could get a whiff of the Pine trees. To this day, I love that smell.

Every year at Christmas our house had the wonderful fragrance from silver tip trees and wreaths, which were from the Pine family.

Unlike the Oaks we passed, as we cruised through the San Joaquin Valley, which stood for the most part alone and separate from the other Oaks, the Pines seemed to love company. To me (having a vivid imagination), they looked like a great green army of trees all standing close together as far as the eye could see. This, of course, is what we call a forest.

California has a wide variety of Pine trees, and elevations dictate where they flourish. The first ones we spotted on our annual trip were the Digger and the Sugar Pines. As we climbed to higher elevations, we began seeing Ponderosas and Lodge Pines.

As a teenager, and into my twenties, I liked fishing for Golden Trout that only live in streams above seven thousand feet. At these upper regions of the Sierras, above timberline where there is more granite rock than soil, you still find Pine trees.

It amazes me how they survive with little to no visible soil and such harsh winters. These tough ones are called the White Bark or Western White Pine. Recently I took a picture of one growing out of the top of a huge granite dome. It was all by itself, and gnarled, and it seemed proud of its ability to survive against all odds. It inspired me to preach a sermon to my church, *All Things Are Possible.*

I guess my favorite of all the Pines that grow here in Northern California is the Ponderosa. This beauty grows around four to six thousand feet in elevation. Most of my Sierra camping from Yosemite to Lake Tahoe and even some hunting trips were at these elevations. (Today my idea of *roughing it* is staying at a Marriott!)

Here's a trivia question: What was the name of the Cartwright's ranch in the T.V. show Bonanza that ran from 1959 to 1973? It was one of my favorite westerns. The Ponderosa was its name.

Unlike the hearty Pines above seven thousand feet, which seem invincible, the Ponderosas have been greatly reduced because of a recent five-year drought in California. More than one hundred million have died from lack of water, which weakens them to the *Beelzebub* of Pine beetles. It's sad to see so many dead trees that once stood strong and healthy.

Over the last forty years, I've seen Christian people get offended with the church, or even disillusioned with God, and uproot themselves from the stream of living water.

It's sad to hear about families who were, once upon a time, healthy, happy church members who slowly die because of a lack of spiritual nourishment.

Like the woman at the well in Samaria, we all need living water:

> "Jesus answered and said to her, "If you knew the gift of God, and who it is who says to you, 'Give Me a drink,' you would have asked Him, and He would have given you living water."
> The woman said to Him, "Sir, You have nothing to draw with, and the well is deep. Where then do You get that living water? Are You greater than our father Jacob, who gave us the well, and

drank from it himself, as well as his sons and his livestock?" Jesus answered and said to her, "Whoever drinks of this water will thirst again, but whoever drinks of the water that I shall give him will never thirst. But the water that I shall give him will become in him a fountain of water springing up into everlasting life." The woman said to Him, "Sir, give me this water, that I may not thirst, nor come here to draw."
— *John 4:10-15*

Let's protect ourselves from offenses and disillusionment, and make sure we continue to drink from the well of living water.

> *Trees are the earth's endless effort to speak to the listening heaven.*

Rabindranath Tagore

THE HOLY TREES OF THE BIBLE
Chapter 7

Two trees that have prominence in the Old Testament are the giant Cedars of Lebanon and the Acacia tree.

" *The righteous shall flourish like a palm tree, he shall grow like a cedar in Lebanon.*" – Psalm 92:12

" *The trees of the Lord are full of sap, the cedars of Lebanon which He planted,*" – Psalm 104:16

" *Then Bezalel made the ark of acacia wood; two and a half cubits was its length, a cubit and a half its width, and a cubit and a half its height. He overlaid it with pure gold inside and outside, and made a molding of gold all around it.*" – Exodus 37:1-2

THE ACACIA

The term *Shittim Wood,* found throughout the Old Testament, is virtually the same as Acacia. Let's first look at the Acacia tree. It's a prized wood. Moses was very familiar with this small, desert-dwelling tree. After all, he grew up in Egypt and spent forty years in the wilderness. The tree became useful to Moses during his time in the desert.

In Exodus, God commanded him to build a moveable tabernacle with the Ark of The Covenant. The Acacia (Shittah) tree was the dominant tree of the region (North Africa). Acacia wood was the only wood used in the structural part of the Tabernacle in the wilderness. It's a hardwood variety, it's bug proof, and its durable properties were perfect for the project. It was a strong and long-lasting wood. God chose this tree and its wood for His tabernacle. The Acacia tree could thrive in a hot, dry place like North Africa, which made its wood iron-like.

Sometimes the Acacia is referred to as *The Wood of God.* I've met Christian leaders who remind me of the Acacia tree. They are not glorious in appearance, or tall as a skyscraper, or even green as a spruce, but they are tough! They've been through it all, and they continue to serve God. No weapon formed against them has ever prospered or taken them out of commission.

I pray that I will be one who stands strong until the end. What an honor it is to be chosen by God to be used in the building of the Ark of the Covenant - Acacia wood overlaid with gold of our Lord Jesus and His humanity, His divinity and glory.

CEDARS OF LEBANON

I love the smell, the look and the feel of Cedar wood. I have it in my closet to scare off the fabric-eating moths and bugs. For some reason they don't like it. Good!

At one time Lebanon had a vast supply of these spectacular Cedars, prized in days past by the Egyptians, Babylonians, Assyrians, Phoenicians, Persians, and yes, the Israelites. Today, if you look at the flag of Lebanon, its logo is the Cedar tree.

King Solomon loved these trees. It was the only wood used in the Temple of God that he built. We sometimes call it *Solomon's Temple*.

The Cedars found in parts of Lebanon are the largest of all Cedars, growing up to one hundred and fifteen feet high, with trunks measuring twelve to fourteen feet in diameter. No wonder Solomon saw these as perfect building materials for the temple.

Today we have found many uses for Cedar oil: hair growth remedy, toothache and gum medicine, and anti-fungal medication, to name a few. No wonder these two trees, the Acacia and the Cedar, are called *Holy Trees*. Both were connected to God's house and His presence.

" But now the Lord my God has given me rest on every side; there is neither adversary nor evil occurrence. And behold, I propose to build a house for the name of the Lord my God, as the Lord spoke to my father David, saying, "Your son, whom I will set on your throne in your place, he shall build the house for My name." Now therefore, command that they cut down cedars for me from Lebanon; and my servants will be with your servants, and I will pay you wages for your servants according to whatever you say. For you know there is none among us who has skill to cut timber like the Sidonians."
— 1 Kings 5:4-6

❝

In nature, nothing is perfect and everything is perfect. Trees can be contorted, bent in weird ways and they're still beautiful.

❞

Alice Walker

THE MONTEREY CYPRESS
Chapter 8

One of the blessings of living where I do, in South San Jose, is that I can be in the Monterey or Carmel-by-the-Sea area in just over an hour. My wife, Carla, and I often drive down just for lunch, which is usually the fresh catch of the day. Between Monterey and Carmel is the famous Seventeen Mile Drive, which is in the beautiful Del Monte Forest. The world-famous Pebble Beach golf course and Cypress Point are also located here.

Arguably the most photographed tree in the world is the must stop, must see, *Lone Cypress*. Over the years we've often taken guest speakers who have come to our church to see this coastal paradise.

The Monterey Cypress only grows here. What is fascinating is how the wind and the salt air help shape these *Bonsai-looking* beauties into almost unworldly figures.

There's the *Ghost tree,* the *Witch tree,* and the one we named the *Alien Tree.* But, none capture the imagination like the *Lone Cypress* in Rocky Point. How this little guy became a West Coast icon is amazing. It's around two-hundred and fifty years old and it has survived storms, the vandalism of a mentally unstable man who tried to burn it down, and other crazy attacks. Nevertheless, bold and beautiful, it's still here.

Companies all over the map use the Lone Cypress as their logo, in one form or another. Its owners – the Pebble Beach Company, have trademarked the image of the tree.

It almost looks like a sentry, gazing out over the Pacific, firmly rooted in solid rock, telling one and all, *"This place is unique and wonderful. Come and enjoy God's goodness."*

Wouldn't it be nice if we Christians could attract the world, to the point that they would want to stop and take a look at the God we serve and see the beauty of our Spirit-filled life in Jesus?

" *Now Peter and John went up together to the temple at the hour of prayer, the ninth hour. And a certain man lame from his mother's womb was carried, whom they laid daily at the gate of the temple which is called Beautiful, to ask alms from those who entered the temple; who, seeing Peter and John about to go into the temple, asked for alms. And fixing his eyes on him, with John, Peter said, "Look at us."* — Acts 3:1-4

> The Tree of Life is growing where the spirit never dies, and the bright light of salvation shines in dark and empty skies.

Bob Dylan

EDEN'S TREES
Chapter 9

"Then God said, "Let the earth bring forth grass, the herb that yields seed, and the fruit tree that yields fruit according to its kind, whose seed is in itself, on the earth"; and it was so. And the earth brought forth grass, the herb that yields seed according to its kind, and the tree that yields fruit, whose seed is in itself according to its kind. And God saw that it was good." — Genesis 1:11-12

> *"The Lord God planted a garden eastward in Eden, and there He put the man whom He had formed. And out of the ground the Lord God made every tree grow that is pleasant to the sight and good for food. The tree of life was also in the midst of the garden, and the tree of the knowledge of good and evil."* — Genesis 2:8-9

There is an old cowboy saying, *"Right out the gate,"* that seems to fit here. In the first and second chapters of the Bible, we see trees — fruit trees, pleasant to the sight and good to eat. Later in Chapter 3, Eve reverses the order: food first, beauty second!

We also see a tree called *The Tree of Life,* and another called *The Tree of Knowledge of Good and Evil.* For centuries man has suggested and debated what these two trees were. I have to admit I also have an opinion or two!

The purpose of the *fruit* of the tree of life was to sustain eternal life on earth, starting with Adam and Eve. What kind of heavenly fruit was on this one centrally located tree?

No one but God and, yes, I guess Adam and Eve, know but it's fun to speculate. Could it have been a unique tree that is nowhere on earth to be found — perhaps a mystical or mythical, *Fountain of Youth*.

Once Adam and Eve fell, they had to be quickly removed from the garden in order to protect mankind from eating of the tree and being condemned to living in a hell-like state forever.

> " Then the Lord God said, "Behold, the man has become like one of Us, to know good and evil. And now, lest he put out his hand and take also of the tree of life, and eat, and live forever"— therefore the Lord God sent him out of the garden of Eden to till the ground from which he was taken. So, He drove out the man; and He placed cherubim at the east of the garden of Eden, and a flaming sword which turned every way, to guard the way to the tree of life."
> — Genesis 3:22-24

Today, we know who the tree of life is, not what it was! It's Jesus!

"Taste and see that the Lord is good."
— Psalm 34:8

THE TREE OF THE KNOWLEDGE OF GOOD AND EVIL

Even though Adam and Eve were placed in paradise where life was good, there still was available to them the tree of bad choices. Life is formed by our choices. I have a little saying, *"Wrong voices, wrong choices. Wrong faces, wrong places."*

Someone might bring up the question, "What's wrong with having knowledge of both what is good and right, and what is wrong or evil?" That seems like a valid question. In fact, many non-believers have challenged me with that question.

Ok, let's unpack it. This passage, like a lot of portions of scripture, deals with *merisms*. It's an expression of *totality by the mention of polarity*. Kind of a *big picture* saying, leaving out the fine print if you will. What God didn't want was for Adam and Eve to know all that is good, as He does, and all that is evil, as He is privy to all knowledge. Man is not God!

Notice Satan's temptation to Eve:

> *"Now the serpent was more cunning than any beast of the field which the Lord God had made. And he said to the woman, "Has God indeed said, 'You shall not eat of every tree of the garden'?" And the woman said to the serpent, "We may eat the fruit of the trees of the garden; but of the fruit of the tree which is in the midst of the garden, God has said, 'You shall not eat it, nor shall you touch it, lest you die.'" Then the serpent said to the woman, "You will not surely die. For God knows that in the day you eat of it your eyes will be opened, and you will be like God, knowing good and evil." — Genesis 3:1-5*

So, what kind of forbidden fruit hung on this tree of prohibition? Again, no one knows, but most agree it wasn't an apple. The poor apple gets blamed for so much. Remember Snow White? Apples appear in many religious traditions — some in a positive light, and others not so positive.

This may be why: in Ancient Greek mythology, there was a story called, *The Golden Apples in the Garden of Hesperides*. In this story, the apple was a symbol of knowledge, temptation, and immortality.

Renaissance painters following this theme began using the apple in their paintings of Adam and Eve's treason.

The confusion of this fruit – the apple – may be due to the similarity of two words in the Latin translation of the Bible, known as the Vulgate. The word *evil* in the tree's name in Latin is *mali*. The word for apple in other places in the Bible (Proverbs 25:11 or Song of Solomon 2:3) is *mala* meaning *bad*.

Our Adam's apple in the larynx of our throat got its name from a folk tale that Adam choked while eating the forbidden fruit because it got stuck in his throat.

No one, of course, knows what kind of fruit it was. Many Rabbis believe and suggest the forbidden fruit was grapes from a grape tree. Their reasons are interesting.

I've heard it was the pomegranate, or a carob, maybe a fig. I could see it being a fig. What did Adam and Eve cover themselves with after they fell? Fig leaves! All this is speculation. Let's not forget, when the Bible is not clear, we shouldn't try to add to it. However, it's fun to let our imagination wander — but not too much.

> *A tree with strong roots laughs at storms.*

Malay Proverb

THE SYCAMINE TREE
Chapter 10

" Take heed to yourselves. If your brother sins against you, rebuke him; and if he repents, forgive him. And if he sins against you seven times in a day, and seven times in a day returns to you, saying, 'I repent,' you shall forgive him." And the apostles said to the Lord, "Increase our faith." So, the Lord said, "If you have faith as a mustard seed, you can say to this mulberry tree, 'Be pulled up by the roots and be planted in the sea,' and it would obey you." — Luke 17:3-6

The Sycamine tree is mentioned only once in the King James version, and it's here in our opening text. In other versions, it's called a *Mulberry tree*. Both are in the *Fig Tree* family. Later, in another chapter, I will discuss the Sycamore tree and its place in the Gospels. In our narrative, Jesus begins by warning His disciples about offenses:

> "Then He said to the disciples, "It is impossible that no offenses should come, but woe to him through whom they do come!" — Luke 17:1

He goes on to teach on forgiveness and that there's no end or reason not to forgive, no matter the offense. Let's face it, it's hard enough to forgive some people once, let alone all day long. Matthew heard this amazing conversation:

> "Then Peter came to Him and said, 'Lord, how often shall my brother sin against me, and I forgive him? Up to seven times?" Jesus said to him, "I do not say to you, up to seven times, but up to seventy times seven." — Matthew 18:21-22

Wow! Now does that mean after four hundred and ninety times (in a day) we forgive, it's enough? No, Jesus is really saying, never stop forgiving. His use of the removal of the Sycamine tree is worth examining. Did you notice in Luke 17:5 the exasperated disciples said, *"Increase our faith." Or, Lord, we are going to need a lot of help doing all this forgiving!* (Don't we all?)

Back to the Sycamine tree: the Sycamine tree was a very tall tree that had a deep root system. Removing one was very difficult. Just cutting down the trunk was not enough. With the roots intact it would live and begin to grow back. It's hard to kill an old Sycamine.

Unforgiveness, likewise, can be so deeply rooted in one's soul, that completely uprooting it is a challenge. Deep roots of unforgiveness produce bitter fruit.

The wood of the Sycamine was used to build coffins and caskets — products of death! I think you see the connection.

The fig, like the fruit of the Sycamine, was extremely bitter and hard to eat. Only poor people dared fill their stomachs with these undesirable figs. Likewise, people who are poor in love, hope, faith, and mercy still prefer the bitter figs over the fruit of the spirit.

Here's one last stunning fact. The Sycamine was unnaturally pollinated. It was, of all things, pollinated by wasps that were attracted to the bitter fruit. Beware! Offenses can sting and hurt all of us. What do we do about it? Do we let bitterness and unforgiveness destroy our lives and poison relationships, or do we obey our Lord?

Don't be a Sycamine tree!

" So, the Lord said, "If you have faith as a mustard seed, you can say to this mulberry tree, 'Be pulled up by the roots and be planted in the sea,' and it would obey you." — Luke 17:6

> We can learn a lot from trees;
> they're always grounded,
> but never stop reaching
> heavenward.

Everett Mamor

THE SYCAMORE TREE
Chapter 11

This beautiful large tree which somewhat resembles our Walnut Tree was called a Valley Tree (Vale), or Lowland Tree.

> *" The king made silver as common in Jerusalem as stones, and he made cedar trees as abundant as the sycamores which are in the lowland."*
> *— 2 Chronicles 9:27*

They didn't do well in the mountains where it was chilly and sometimes snowed.

> *"He destroyed their vines with hail, and their sycamore trees with frost." — Psalm 78:47*

That's why one of my favorite stories in the Bible happens in the city of Jericho, which is 846 feet below sea level — perfect for Sycamores. Jericho, the *city of palms*, had many of the shade-giving beauties and lined many streets and paths with them.

Now, on to our story:

> *"Then Jesus entered and passed through Jericho. Now behold, there was a man named Zacchaeus who was a chief tax collector, and he was rich. And he sought to see who Jesus was, but could not because of the crowd, for he was of short stature. So, he ran ahead and climbed up into a sycamore tree to see Him, for He was going to pass that way. And when Jesus came to the*

place, He looked up and saw him, and said to him, "Zacchaeus, make haste and come down, for today I must stay at your house." So, he made haste and came down, and received Him joyfully." — Luke 19:1-6

Without a doubt, Zacchaeus was the most hated man in Jericho. Zacchaeus was a Jew who worked for Rome, and his responsibility was to extract heavy taxes from the citizens of that region, which included his fellow Jews. While doing so, he also lined his pockets. He was not just a tax collector, like Matthew. He was a chief tax collector! He heard about Jesus, and his curiosity got the best of him. He tried to get a peek at this new prophet from Galilee.

Of course, no one was going to let him cut in front of him or her to give him a roadside view. But he came up with a *short man* plan. He ran ahead of the parade and climbed a tree — a big, beautiful Sycamore tree. His experience in that tree changed his life forever.

I wouldn't mind being called a Sycamore tree — a tree that will stoop to the lowest of humanity and lift them to get a glimpse of Jesus our Savior. Let them climb my revelation and sit on branches of mercy and grace and find eternal life.

> "But when they saw it, they all complained, saying, "He has gone to be a guest with a man who is a sinner." Then Zacchaeus stood and said to the Lord, "Look, Lord, I give half of my goods to the poor; and if I have taken anything from anyone by false accusation, I restore fourfold." And Jesus said to him, "Today salvation has come to this house, because he also is a son of Abraham; for the Son of Man has come to seek and to save that which was lost." — Luke 19:7-10

"Blessed is the man who walks not in the counsel of the ungodly, nor stands in the path of sinners, nor sits in the seat of the scornful; but his delight is in the law of the Lord, and in his law he meditates day and night. He shall be like a tree planted by the rivers of water, that bring forth its fruit in its season, whose leaf also shall not wither; and whatever he does shall prosper."
— Psalm 1:1-2

CONCLUSION
Chapter 12

What kind of tree are you? How about your friends? Family? Coworkers? Boss? Children? It's fun to think about, isn't it? But more than fun, it's a Biblical truth. As the Bible says in Isaiah 61:3, we are to be *"...trees of righteousness, the planting of the Lord, that He might be glorified."*

Beginning with Adam, God's assignment to man hasn't changed: *"Then the Lord God took the man and put him in the garden of Eden to tend and keep it."* Genesis 2:15

Productive fruit trees don't just happen spontaneously; they're groomed. Fruit trees need to be cultivated, fertilized, watered, and pruned. Let's be good gardeners, or husbandmen, and remain strong, healthy, and fruitful.

I could go on and on talking about all the various scriptures and varieties of trees hoping to provoke thought and dialogue, but I think through these metaphors you get the picture. I hope this little book blessed you, and the next time you see a beautiful tree, you are inspired to become *Like a Tree.*